To my mother, Siva.

List of Illustrations

C O N T E N T S

Changing

I escape in verse. There I am light. Each poem becomes a master tree in my garden, growing and blooming thoughts into the air, attracting all senses of creativity, and uniting them all together in a simple way, so I can feel without having to solve any social questions. I can look in to myself now and become mindful of my own existence.

Almost like if I was weaving myself into the future and these blind words, were the gentle and soothing hands, creating and holding it all together. I thought of this, and wanted to share it every day.

When I write, I rest. I like to travel back and forth looking at moments that changed my path, and adding to them the outlook of the present. Creating a key, in the form of art, that is able to unlock my own gap of time and consciousness. Plus, I have seen a pattern in myself to stray from all concrete forms of expression, leaving less room for judgement, and more for details.

When I started to play in this intense playground of emotions and realized how sensitive life really is, without having to jump into any mental mud, or raw thoughts and also at the same time, being able to read so many moments together so fully back to back, that I myself have fallen in love with this medium.

There are times too, that I write for intervals yet to arrive. Creating poems that will enhance them when they do. Giving me the opportunity to decide which lines will bring me closer to myself, or someone closer to me. Let it be a lullaby for a child I have yet to bare, or the loss of a friend, or even words of wisdom when my own life seems lost, or the welcome of a love re-visited, and, of course, acceptance of those never to return.

I needed to be true to myself, not sometimes, but always. Holding back would only prove me wrong. I also want to add that the illustrations have a simple meaning that I wanted to share. The black symbolizes the solid sense of myself and the red symbolizes my feelings or the feelings of the art for that matter.

Every moment is a part of us. When we share these moments, let it be simply by saying thank you to a stranger or touching someone we love with a kind word, we are sharing the most precious moments of our lives together without even considering an outcome. I like to look at my poetry and expressions in this sense, and changing is a gift. Enjoy.

-Lady Lee Andrews

In my rough beauty
unadorned...

I'm a ghost

I'm a flower

I'm the spirit essence

Of a dream...

Responding

With you
The morning whispers.
The sun sighs, and
The dew drops.

With you
The inference of love
Is so, that, like time
It never stops.

It's you.
Falling like the rain
Inside my soul.
My pain subsides
Then dies.
I know
The unconditional
Responding.

Like one would, as I
Your kiss. And I,
As Night is longing
Won't miss
To place each loving wish
Upon a star
When your lips
From mine afar
And feel to come again.

Thoughts in the Forest

Love should be as fresh as the morning
And as soft as the night.
Love should be like the water, clear and
As open as the stars are bright
Strong to wish upon.

I look into the stream.
Dry leaves are floating by.
The singing in the forest
Echoes with the rain
And I
Can't stop hearing it run
Softly through the trees
Wishing for me to follow.

True Love protects itself
Unlike any other ghost by its name.
The body is just a treasure chest.
The Spirit is the gain.

When love is put together I feel
The world is not the same
Anymore

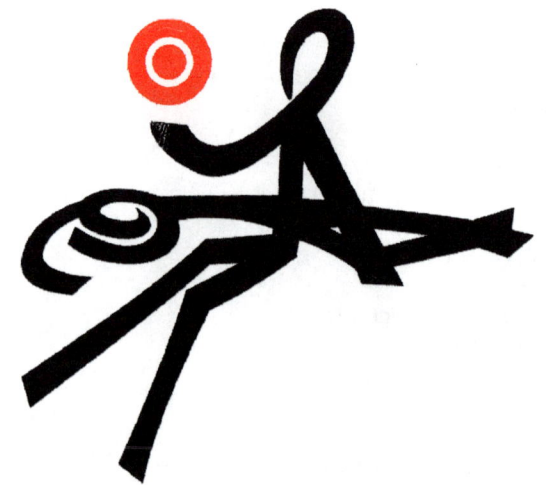

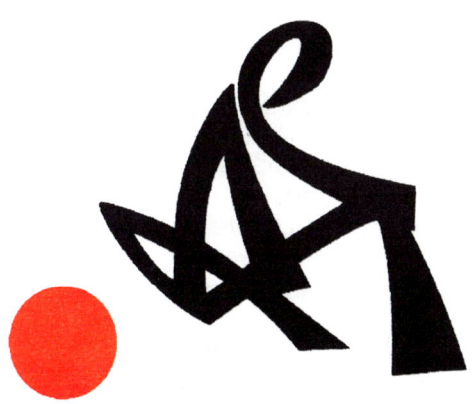

11

Little by Little

I'm letting go
Little by little, but I am.
It sometimes hurts.
I sometimes cry.
I sometimes erase it all
And sometimes I try
And I can't.
But I'm letting go.
I am.
That's just the way I am.
I can't help it anymore.

My mind races
Unlike the hare
Who had patience
To compete.
I'm racing to defeat myself.
It's torture in a shell
My heart has been to hell
I'm letting go.
Little by little, but I am.
I learned that now I can.
Sometimes it's good.
Sometimes it's sweet.
There are times too
That I never meet a standard.
Where questions flow
unanswered
And it's okay in itself
I'm taking down the shelf
Of expectations
Crowded by imitations.
I learned that now I can.

I'm letting go, little by little,
But I am.

Sky Light

Twilight rising
Hypnotizing
Day gently into night.
Moon Sonata.
Star Regatta.
Our wind winding
Waves of light

Freshly Touched

Freshly touched after the shower.
The water falling from the sky,
Rushing down the river every hour.
The stones unaware of all passing by
Yellow, green and in between
The trees are summoned by the light
Orange, blue, a dreamers hue
The cliff beyond the edge of sight.

No One Saw

What joy.
What a sensual joy.
Deliberate-
In to it.
Fear as soft
As sensitive
When your whole body
Feels the pain
When pleasure has reached the brim
And pours
All over
Your senses.

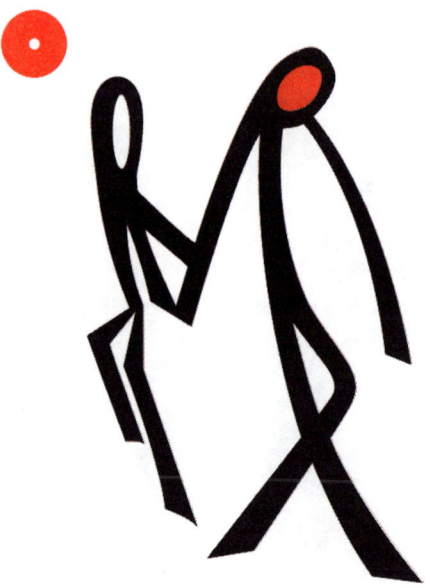

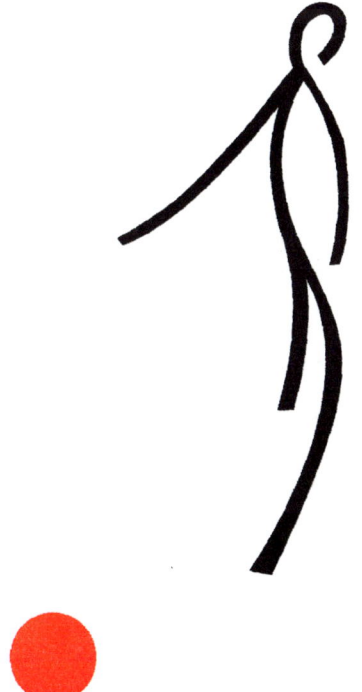

Your Dreams Arrived

Your dreams arrived
At my window.
I unveiled your thoughts.
I heard along
Each line
Feather light
And soft
A melody
Of love
Which found
Its destiny.

Bridges

I fly through the sky.
Loose and free.
Then I fall like a feather,
Reaching for the sea.
Holding every breath that's left in me
I plunge into the depths for my destiny.

After awhile, a hook is ready to take me away.
But I'm afraid, for the bait
Is different today
For it's a dark smile
With a warning kiss
Reaching to take
The breath left in my lips

I look ahead.
My sight is clear.
Someone shot
The killing spear

Through my heart
Its taking my soul
Making me a part
Of the depths real slow.

I feel the salty pain
Cold throughout my body
So fast my fingers
Try to reach
With little time to spare
The crust that separates
This water from the air

I reach out
And grab a hold
A piece of solid hope
and the air pulls me out
As if strangled
By a rope

Another rush
Runs through me fast
The breath of life I know at last.

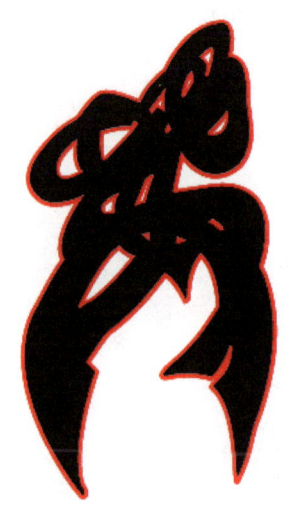

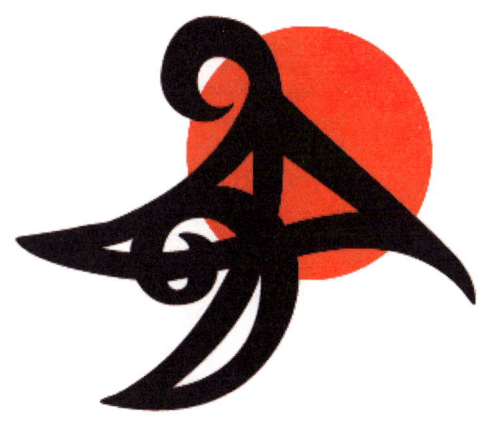

Once

Sing
If you whisper
My name.
Cry
If you do it
In vain.
Kiss me once

Forever.

Lover Lover by the Sea

Lover Lover by the sea
Shadows saying follow me
Footsteps playing with the waves
Watching how the sand behaves
I love you. I, love you.

Cold, so cold so cold so cold
But the moon is full and you are bold
Playing under a spell of happiness
With you everything exists
I love you. I, love you.

My Garden

I'm a swollen rose
In a bed of wheat
Petals so soft of
A color made sweet.

I bloom with the touch
Of breath in the air
My dew from inside
Of time unaware.

I'm a swollen rose
Of sensual descent
Arousing lovers
With my garden scent

Mother Made a Jewel

Mother made
A jewel of me
The day that
I was born.

She loved
The diamond
In the rough-
The rose
Before the thorn.

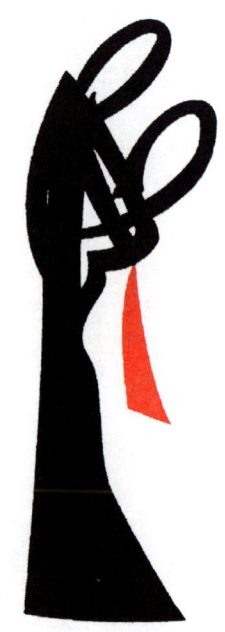

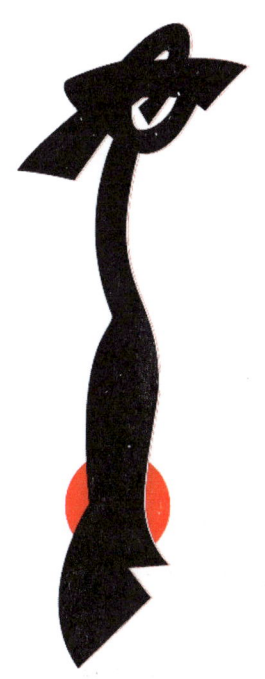

I Am Loving You

Rock like the moon.
Sail like the sea.
Dance like the stars.
Unlock the key.
Give it to me.

Dream like the clouds.
Flow like the wind.
Feel like the water.
No resistance.

Don't wonder where you are now
Think only of me.
Love will appear
If you let go of fear,
And your soul will let go
And be free

Here there is no conclusion.
Options persist.
Dreams cant resist
Their illusions
Of reality,
Anymore than I can
Look away from you,
And not feel
Your love's sensuality,
Becoming on it's own
A fountain in your absence,
When I thirst to taste
The life of your essence again!

Each second seems so far away
Eternity fading forever.
No survivor has returned, they say
To tell of their love's endeavor.

Life becomes so dry sometimes
And tears maybe, the only sign of rain
Nevertheless I have seen
The light in all our love and what it means.
And, that's the world to me.

Baby B

I'm just a baby
Rocking in love
It's those clouds
Above me
That I'm dreaming of-

Each with an Angel
Singing Good night.

The wind blows
My eyes close.
And I know
I'll sleep tight.

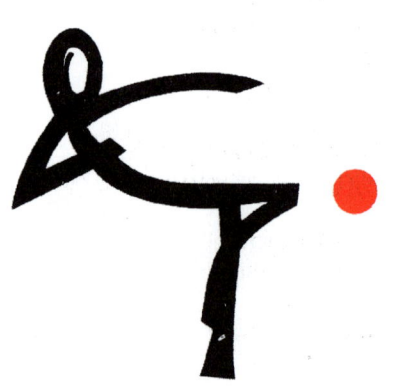

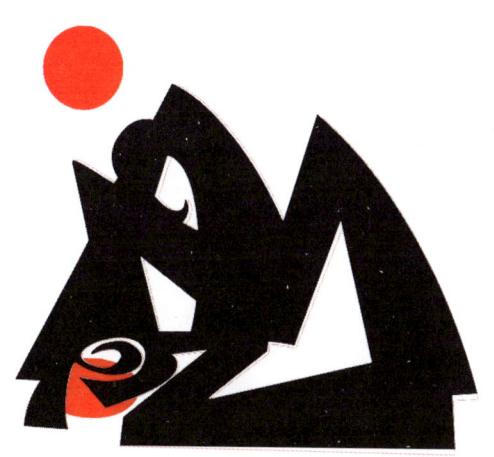

Dear Dreamer

I knew my eyes were open.
I heard the whispers say
A wish was to be given
That I was to give away

My wonder and my praise
To find all this life, this awareness, around me
A daze, preparing me to make it come true.

It was enlightening.

I would assist the Meaning
My hand would be providing my
Life as a means of relaying the truth.

My heart was washed.
And tickled.

I could feel the essence suddenly inside me
And resting on my lips, the faith of Love
Awaiting my chosen call.

If so could be said, a frosty mist. Soft, and crisp
Sharp celestial chimes swaying in harmony.
A motion creating peace from side to side.

I was touched, blessed.

Then you, unseen, I found were to be my honor.
The bridge of dreams rose from the depths
Of reality for me to cross
I was overwhelmed.
I felt like I was floating,
Yet my steps were as soft as snow
Falling from the sky,
Purling a trail behind me
I reached you then-
Your beauty as soft as your skin.
I knew not such a gentle face in days of open sight!
Nor will I see in your eyes the wish I will tonight-

Dear dreamer,
Your soul has kept a secret well, your desire runneth
deep
And the angels made a promise long ago, which I am
here to keep.
This wish upon my lips is yours.
With pleasure I bestow
And when you rise,
You will awake
With my miracle.

Wind Light

Wind light
Sailing flame
Waves like rivers
From the rain.
Watch the fall
Form and grow

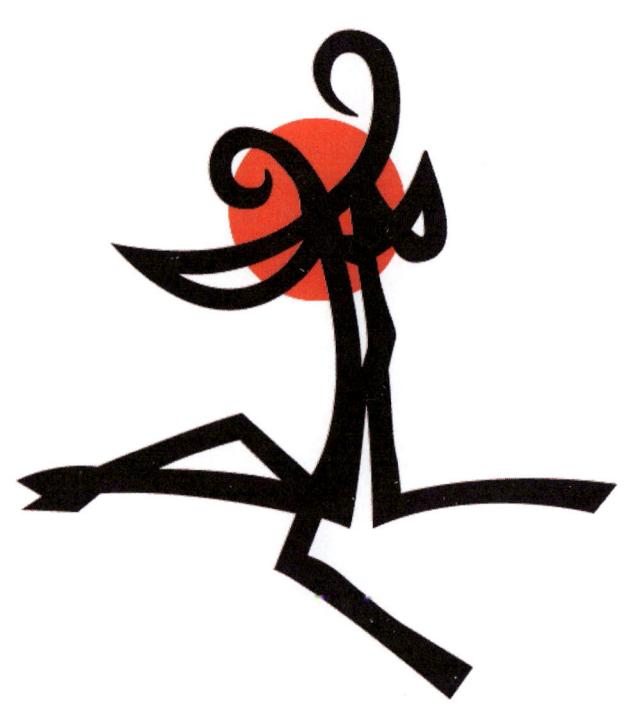

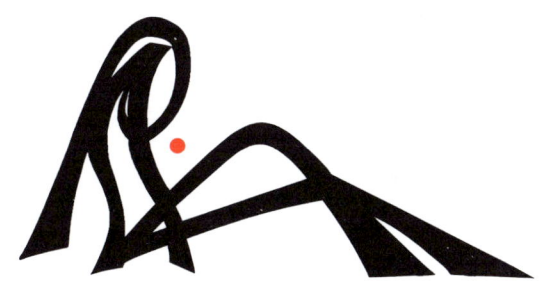

Today

Today
Is the tip
Of the mountain
And the straw
On tomorrow's
Back.

Inside (I am Beautiful)

I am beautiful.
The wind has shaped my face
The sun brought forth my soul
Each step I gave, another was made
Unconditional

Thank God.
Dreams denied have never died.

In my heart I'm blooming
Pursuing butterflies

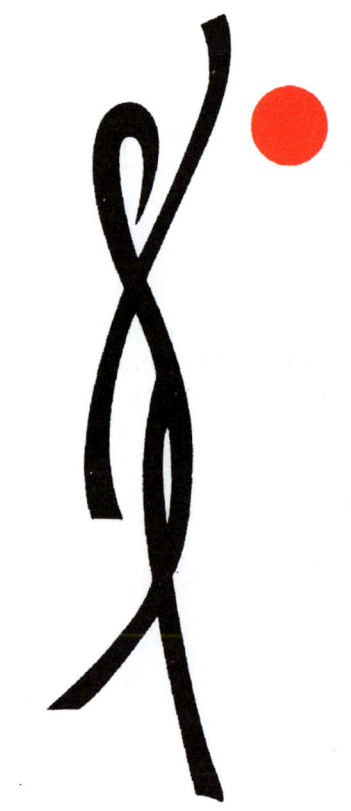

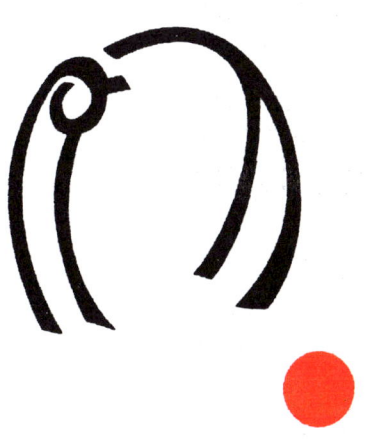

It's Valentine's

I hear a part of me saying
Please don't go.
It's like my body is not hearing
Me telling it no.
But I'm not here to talk about
Dimensions
We're all afraid of being mentioned
And denied.
It's Valentine's.
It's Valentine's, and I want
To talk about Love.

If I had my heart over to give
I'd wrap it in the ocean
String it with the stars
Make a bow of light
And write
On the
Moon...
You are my Valentine.
My sweet devotion lies within you
forever!
My lips and lashes
Will sign with a kiss

If I had my heart over
I would do this
For you
My Valentine.

Love

[Kiss.]

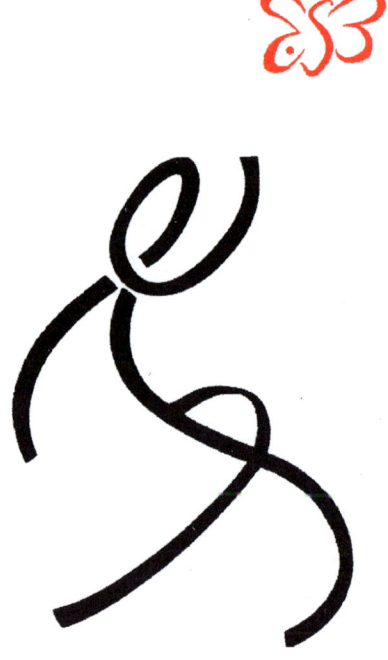

Moments

My breast, below your skin
Feels caressed
As I feel the wind
Run to your heart
With all my kiss within,
Each others arms

Each time I open my eyes
I am dreaming.
To look upon you is like breathing
In my life.

And to know my body's rest
Will lay here undressed through the
night
I hold you closer.
All ties undone
Where two are one
I hold you closer.

On the dark side of my dreams
The stars and common things
We do not know
Appear with perfect clarity

Details

Hear the bass
In the waves
Now rocking.
Feel the drums
In the sky.
Now, shocking
Strings sound,
Like a chorus breeze
Now
Caught in the voice of air

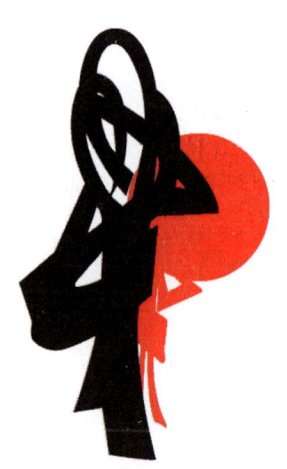

Love Becomes a Mother

Your soft voice at times
Gave me strength.
Your silence, by peace,
Let me go.
Did you know now
To call me as you did
With such authority
That I cried
In your arms
When I could not listen.

Your soft voice at times
Gave me sorrow.
Your dreams would slip
Through your heart
So fragile, so premature.
"Let me live although I won't endure"
They seemed to say, drowned by
The sweet taste of
Rum and wine.

All of you becomes me
Like my brothers.
And my sister, you chose
With time.
I will keep your secrets
In the eyes you adored.
If by reason, time or need
They open unto me,
I will receive them.
Unlike my heart
Which never knew

Love becomes a mother
Once she's gone.

If I a Statue

If I a statue
With such a pose
My soul would still
Shatter if you
Were to come close.
My new heart
And armor
Would disappear
Although of Marble
To you I'd appear.

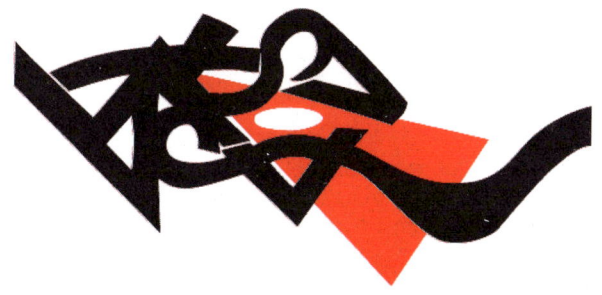

There is a Fire

There is a fire, in the forest, of my soul
And rain is about to come.
Betrayal is in the air of life
And you see,
What pain has done
And tears cannot become
A consolation anymore.

You know the way
But you closed the door.
Left the key on the other side!
Shadows live upon the floor
From the light you cannot hide.

Aware of what? You plead again,
As you realize who you are,
And, each time you cry to run away
The mirror is not that far.

The fire, blue in its horizon,
Eliminates my power.
My heart fights to regain control
While I stand and cower
In the truth.

Almost Lost

Almost lost
With no desire
To return.
If my hope
Is in the fire
Let it burn.

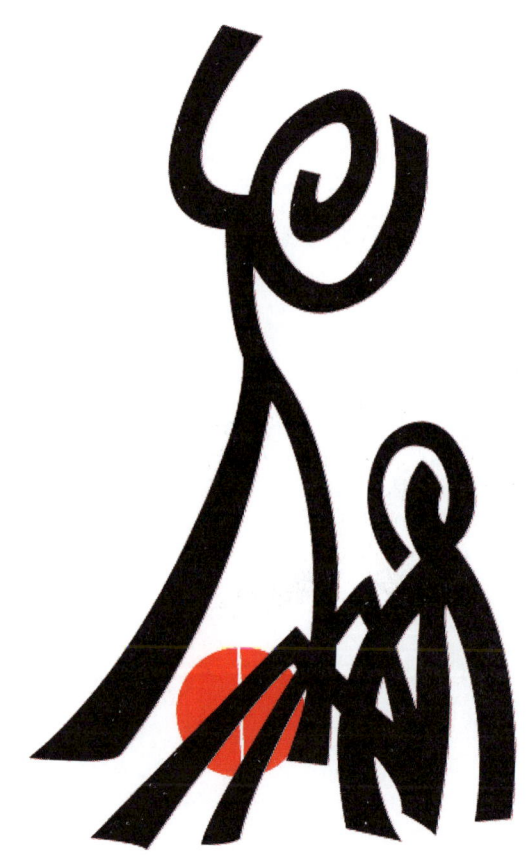

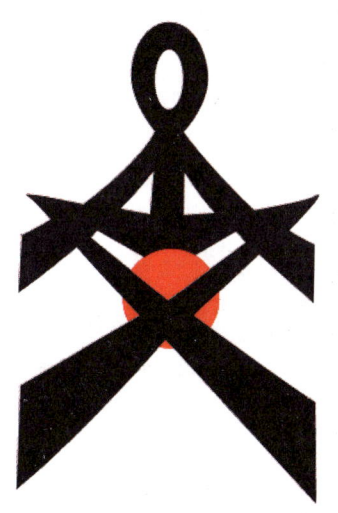

As Children

The weight of change
Defies the law
Honoring the system
That we saw
As children.

The world was more
Than this to me.
I was not ready
But now that's how
We see
As children.

Father, home is
Not your place.
Mother, cover
Now your face.
Tell him please to go.

I didn't mean
For tears to rise.

I'm glad sometimes
That everything dies
You know...
That's why we change
As children.

Just Checking

Grapes and bread
And Cheerios.
Hungry Jack,
And Oreos,
Goober Grape,
Sugar, cream cheese,
A gallon of milk,
Pickles and peas.
One dozen eggs,
A half bag of ice
Eight frozen buns
And bacon? Suffice.

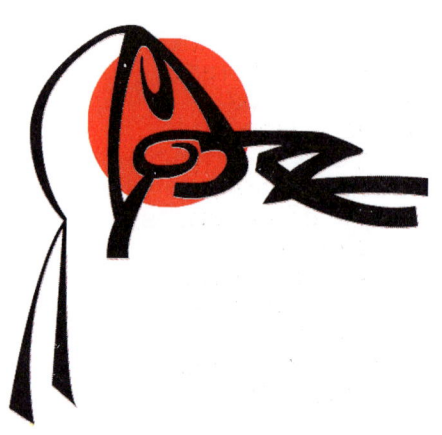

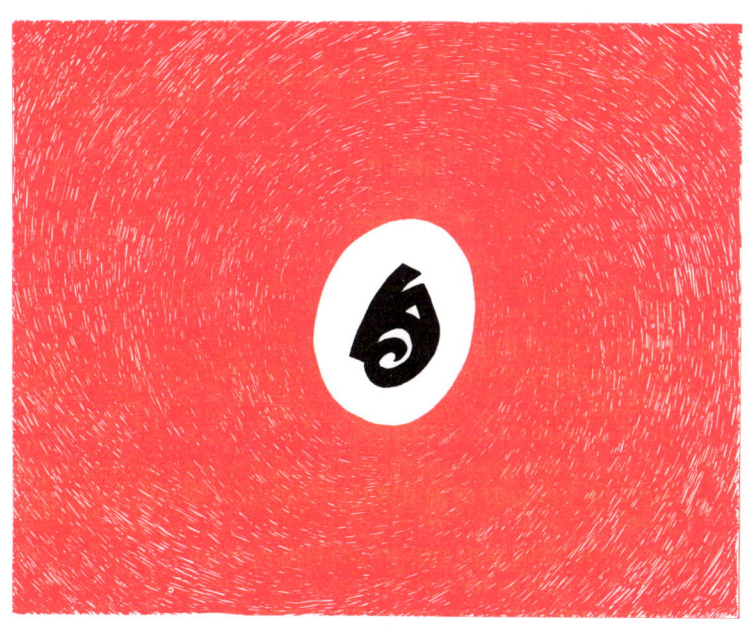

Water Well to Stress Bucket

Some of my sweetest thoughts are
Waiting to
Refresh you.
Haven't you ever heard of the "Horse
And The Water" syndrome?
Or, silly, do you keep the window closed,
When
The love you let go
Comes back to claim it's yours?

You are as blind as a bat in the sun
You need to hibernate. You would be
Kicked out
Of hell for being so cold.
Smile once in a while, will ya?
Who said you had to drop everything?
That is
Just a sign of insecurity.

And I'll tell you one thing, once you get it,
Self-
Confidence, you never go back. And
I'm not going to carry anyones baggage,
Because they are afraid to let their
Feelings go.
I love to fly, and I love to drink fresh
Water.

Open Fire

Does he really miss
These moments time?
Does he hear my name
In the pouring wine?
Does he laugh
And promise to share
All the moments
Wished I was there?
Do you know?

Sugar white candle
Sunny stream
Am I now his only dream?
Do you know?

Does he count the second
As an hour?
Do you know if it is our
Destiny
To think of each this way?
Do you know?
Does he love me?

Open Fire
Execute my
Last desire
If not
True.

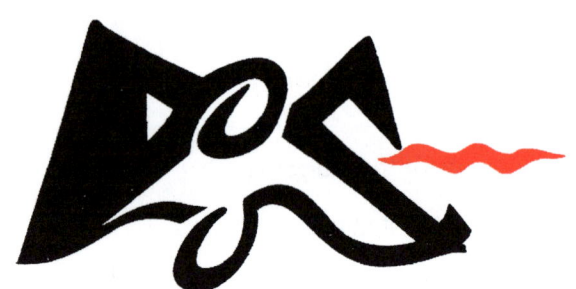

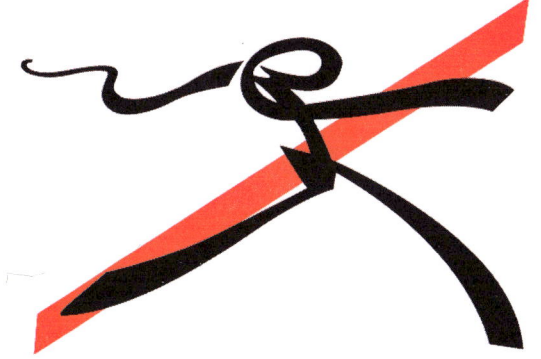

Only the Wind

Only the wind
Can see my
Love for you.

The fallen petal
Knows my
Pain

Black Cherry Eyes

Black cherry eyes
My lover.
Rum-rose honey lashes
Upon a hazel bed,
Sunshine vanilla soft
And the dreams
Within
Are said
With each Desired kiss
Against my lips
Caressed.
Each hidden need
To have me
Then confessed
My lover
Knows me well.
I feel the passion
Sweet and strong.
I feel the love in me
Belong
As if his dreams
Were coming true
As if everything
To him-
Was you!
His gentle flavor
Leads you into him.
Don't fight
You cannot win.
I know
My lover well.

I Can't

Love can't come into my halo.
It's deep and sad, and broken too.
With me you thirst
If you need water.
With me you fall
If you need space
Your essence seeps into the air
Like a spell
A sweet perfume
So faint that I can' t follow
Or have this love I need
From you.
With me you are airless
Under water
With me our dreams
Cannot embrace
With me your pain
Is so much stronger
With me your love
Cannot be traced
Love can't come into my halo
It's deep and sad, and lonely too—
When you make me feel
That I belong
In all that' wrong
For you.

I Fell like a Kite

I fell
Like a kite
Cut from the wind
As if all my life
Had been
Hanging on a string
And someone

Let it go.

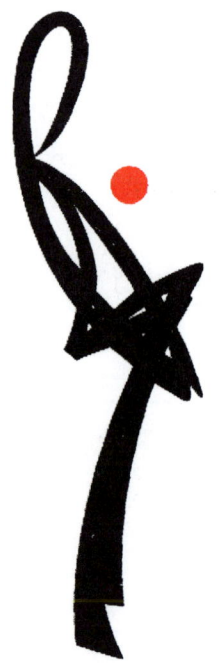

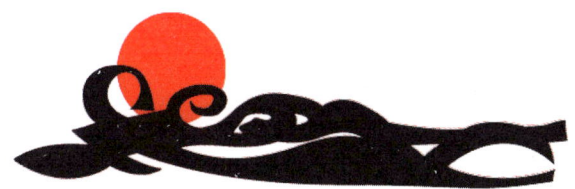

In the Line of Fire

Does it hurt
To see me this way?
I'm really
Really sorry.
My heart was on the line
Please convert your feelings
And head them towards mine
To understand.

I had to stand this way
In front of you.
Justify all reasons
Face our equal rights
Qualify what's true
With nothing
Except
Who stands by me
Who will it now be
Since money owns it all

Regardless, heartless
One can still survive
But sometimes
Not alive.

How sad to make me feel
So young that one can die
Within someone who showed them
How to love.

I Blink

I

Blink

Through

The eyes

Of a

Bird.

By The River

I remember
You left me
By the river.
The spider web.
Looked threatening
A shade of gold so light
A silver.
Lines across each other...
You left me
For another
I was lost-

How can I explain?
The water to the rain
My heart to the flow
That seemed to pass?
How could one exist?
Without the other
Co-exist?
For neither knows how long
They'll last.

How can I tell my love
That soon you will be of
The past?
I remember you left me by the river
I was lost.

Yes

No more Beauty
Could be said
But seen, and touched,
Then felt.
We, unlike ourselves,
Have met,
Where, each other
Dwelt.

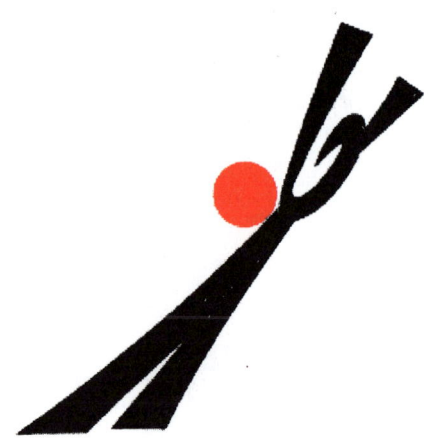

74

Let Me Go

I shouldn't have to learn
To say no,
When I love, I let it go.
All familiar faces
Blur and mix.
Tell me who you are
When both affix
And leave me blind
With joy.
Teach me truth
And nothing more.
Take my youth
Please, I beg- before,
You close the door
And leave me alone
No longer believing
In my own
Desires.
Leave my body alone.
It's an illusion.
It's not an offering
Something to be sacrificed
To show my true devotion.
Respect my peace
Like one respects the ocean.

Glances

Your heart wanted
To know me
Your words
Didn't let it show.
The only thing
We share now
Is what
We didn't let go

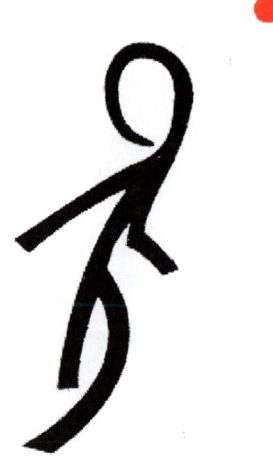

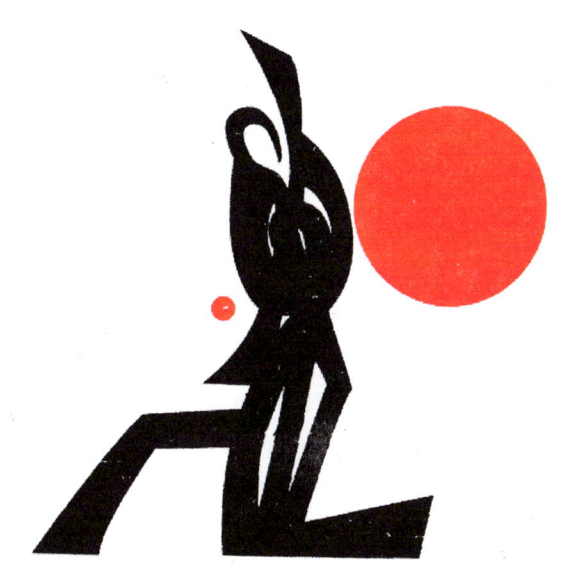

I Feel a Man Upon Me

I feel a man upon me, listening to my soul
Like water pouring over the edge, when my cup is
Full.
He does not know he touches me, he dreams
So wide-awake.
He feels I do not know him. My true actions
I forsake.
Pure, sharp notes allure me. Desire sings within
Like madness.
I capture the beast inside me
To eliminate
My sadness.
Cold words from the fire, a cross between life,
And death-
My voice will starve to love, before
I give up what's left.
He has no keys to open my senses.
He has no need to owe his pain.
He is sentenced by my past denials, and pays
Deeply to pertain.
Someone else will whisper. Someone else will cry.
Someone else will soothe his loneliness,
Because, now
I refuse to try.
Love can't lure me, nor barriers break.
Or when in doubt in silence fake.
I see a man before me, and, he is
Letting me go.
Not in least a feeling of me, no "unconditional"
One last chance he gives me,
No quality in choice.
An ultimatum story
Where others now
Revoice.

Sometimes

I picture thoughts
Behind that hidden wall.
Darkness in a battle of lights
And fire
I felt if I opened my eyes
I would fall
Exposed again to life,
Desire.
Closed.
I kept them closed.

My soul began its motion.
My heart played in every song.
My body, as my spirit, sang.
And my mind did love no wrong.

I became unknown
In your arms
Your love
Was all I knew

You will deny what you cannot see
You will regret what you cannot feel
The loss, you know, is unrepairable.
When Love pleads guilty
For being unreal.

Confessions

My Love looks directly into me.
I witness within, my Innocence
Pleading for my Heart to be true.

Love Rising

You placed my naked body
At the bottom of the stairs
Luring me to rise and seek
What every lover shares

I rose softly, almost cold,
My body had to shiver
Feeling every sensual shock
Each step had to deliver.

So fresh my senses soon became
Aware that life, was not the same.
I closed my eyes to feel again.
Risking all, but I ascend!

I became another motion in space
Unaware of it's own existence.

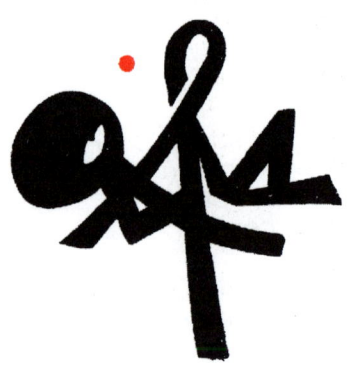

84

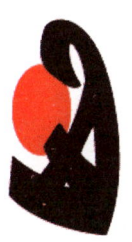

The First Story

.

What?
You think
The love of your life
Is going to have
A clean sheet?
I'm tired
Of keeping you
Updated.
How many men
Does it take
To destroy
One woman?
How many women
Does it take
To make
One man?
And don't you dare
Begin to try me.
I've been a part of you
As much as you have
Been apart from me.
Give yourself to the world my dear
I
Can't
Keep up
With your
Digressions
Anymore.

A Friend's Will

Something is hurting me inside
And I don't know what it is.
From my body so much pain can hide
But not from one like this

I rock in silence by my shore
I think of never and evermore
I stare, ignore what's there
Listen for an answer to come.
And nothing soothes my ocean blues

But I wait, for someone
Is listening
To what I have to say
Waiting another day
For me to open like the sky
And be myself again.

Black Out

All cantankerous foes and follies
Filled with vintage blows
And swollen bodies
Bursting thunder
My joy asunder!
Pardy those who will forget
That life still owns the victims yet.

Red Rose Velvet

Red Rose Velvet
Lying on the ground.
Who did she last see?

Porcelain Beauty
Lips without a sound.
Dreaming now for free

Who was he?
Who was he?

Be-holder, what
Were you looking for
That her life couldn't keep?

The Jewel is lost.
Petals on the floor,
Like her last heart beat.

Who was he?
Who was he?

Thoughts

So many abandoned houses
Next to busy
City streets.
Naming not the homeless
Yet
That each
Tomorrow greets.
I look in awe
And tend to fill them
With my daily dreams.

Turning Away

If I could wash away my memories
If they could only sink into the ground
If I could leave them behind, like I've
Done so much,
Where they can Never be found.

This will answer all my questions
When love is absent, so is truth.
I won't remember my heart as broken
By the terrible cross of my youth.

And you
Denied me, quoted your life over and
Over.
You despised me, but not
Before you told me it's over.
No intentions of emotions mentioned at
All
What we saw had nothing in common.
You took me down
Into the darkness of your desires.
Left me with no way out .

Sorry love, if this hurts,
But I can't see beyond this illusion
Anymore.
If you keep coming like this,
How can I open my door?

Will time ever cease
To remind me of how bad it hurts?

Red Needle

Red Needle
Thread or Shot.
Piercing, filling
The life I got.

One saves, one feels,
One writes, one kills,
Part of a
Perfect thought.

The Song of Poetry

An ovation
Each Time
The waves
Fell on my words.

Against the rocks
They hit
So clearly

And the flying of birds
Singing 'bye,
Gave an air
Of delight,

And the sky
Was forever.

I read like a dream.
Each poem like a stream
That flowed like
The life within me

It seemed
So simple

To express nothing less
To exist as the best
I can be.

With no choice to accept
What nature has kept
Part of me.

Special Thanks, For Unlimited Suppo and Trust.

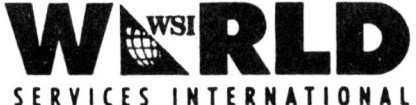

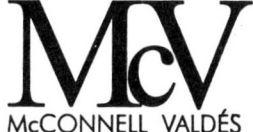

McCONNELL VALDÉS

*

When someone believes in you,
Reaching for the best is just a
Breath away.
Under God, I thank you
For being who you are
In my life, with all my heart.
And for requesting
Nothing
In return, but my
Happiness.

L,L.L